Music Makes a Difference

M&K Publishing a part of M&K Update Ltd
© 2007, M&K Update Ltd.

Music Makes a Difference
A practical guide to developing music sessions with people with learning disabilities
Author: Dr Toni Bunnell
ISBN: 978-1-905539-19-2

First published 2007

British Library Catalogue in Publication Data
A catalogue record for this book is available from the British Library

To contact M&K Publishing write to:
M&K Update Ltd • The Old Bakery • St. John's Street • Keswick • Cumbria • CA12 5AS
Tel: 01768 773030 • Fax: 01768 781099
publishing@mkupdate.co.uk
www.mkupdate.co.uk

Printed in United Kingdom

Music Makes a Difference

A Practical Guide to developing music sessions
with people with learning disabilities

Toni Bunnell

For my father, John Bunnell,
who through his exceptional ability
to play the piano and compose tunes,
opened my eyes to the
world of music.

ACKNOWLEDGEMENT
All the information provided in the section on home-made instruments in Chapter 5
is taken from Alex Whinnom's book, Let's Make Music, Printforce 1989.

NOTE
Throughout this work the terms 'therapist', 'leader' and 'group leader' are synonymous.

Contents

About the author

Toni Bunnell has lectured in physiology in the Faculty of Health, Hull University since 1994. She is currently engaged in research in the field of chemical and sensory ecology. Toni gained a BSc in zoology in 1970, an MSc in medical biochemistry in 1972 and completed a PhD in animal behaviour in 1982. She taught for many years in schools in Britain before living in Germany between 1980 and 1983 where she worked with a scientific publisher. On her return to Britain she concentrated on establishing herself once more as a musician and returned to secondary teaching and later lecturing in further and higher education.

An accomplished musician and song writer, Toni Bunnell has appeared many times on radio and television and, while living in Heidelberg, was a member of the German band Distelbaum. She has also produced several cassettes and CDs of songs and one of hurdy gurdy tunes, as well as illustrated song sheets and a song book. She has undertaken many bookings in folk clubs, art centres, and folk festivals. Toni writes her songs on a variety of themes and accompanies herself on the Appalachian dulcimer, guitar and harmonium, the hurdy gurdy and fiddle being played for tunes from the Celtic tradition.

'All Over England' is a musical show written and presented by Toni and incorporates her songs and slides. With inherent educational value, it encourages communication and audience participation. It has been performed in schools, centres for people with mental health problems, day centres for elderly people with mental health problems, and hospital wards, and has toured in Germany and Austria.

It was through music that Toni came into increased contact with people with learning disabilities and began working with them on a weekly basis in a hospital for five years. Her work there was with an occupational therapy department group and with two groups of people presenting challenging behaviour. She also ran regular sessions at a number of other venues, for both adults and children with learning disabilities, in community houses, schools, and Gateway clubs. This book is based on her experience and intends to provide practical advice to other music session leaders who, like her, may not necessarily be trained music therapists.

Introduction

The aim of this book is to inspire people to set up music groups with people who have various levels of learning disability, including those displaying challenging, disturbed and/or destructive behaviour. Music has been shown to be of indisputable value when dealing with people with learning disabilities. Although still viewed dubiously in some quarters, this book presents a case for using music extensively with people with learning disabilities.

With the rare exception, most books dealing with music for people with learning disabilities seem to consider only those who are fairly able, of a pleasant disposition and who rarely exhibit challenging behaviour. However, music can also be extremely important when dealing with people who display challenging behaviour. In fact music can be used to influence such behaviour for the better. It is unfortunate that those people who would probably benefit most from a music session are often excluded from occupational therapy activities, such as music sessions, by virtue of their anti-social behaviour. This problem can be overcome by seeing such people on their own in small groups. I hope the fact that I am not by training a music therapist will help to encourage other people who have the inclination and the will to succeed, but not the official training, to establish music groups with adults with learning disabilities: it is enthusiasm, the desire to learn, and above all the aptitude to work with adults with learning disabilities that come first and foremost.

It is of great value, though not essential, to be able to play one or two musical instruments. Here again, a professional level of attainment is hardly important. More important is the capability to organise music sessions to suit individual needs, the flexibility to change certain aspects of the sessions when necessary and the ability to help each individual within a group achieve their full potential through music.

For those people who presently do not play a musical instrument, several books (some with CDs) can be obtained and will serve the dual purpose of providing varied material tailor-made for singing and group participation, as well as instant music. Further guidelines with regard to different instruments etc. are given in Chapter 5.

ADVICE FOR THOSE WORKING WITH PEOPLE WITH LEARNING DISABILITIES

- Remember that people with learning disabilities are human beings who should be treated with the same respect as any other person and that they have emotions and feelings just like anyone else.
- Try to avoid talking about clients whilst in their presence. They often understand a lot more than we give them credit for.
- Your behaviour will be watched closely by the clients, many of whom are great mimics.
  Please bear this in mind. Be yourself, but your best self.
- When working with people with learning disabilities you are in a position to help them expand on things they can do. Do not dwell on things they cannot do.
- Never set a person with learning disabilities a task that they cannot reasonably do. A sense of failure can be very damaging, whereas an achievement, however small, can be a great source of pleasure.
- Never be afraid to seek advice from the people who have regular contact with clients. You will not be treated as 'stupid' but rather as 'sensible' for such actions.
- Do not make promises to the clients that you cannot keep, for example, if you are not sure if you will be visiting the centre next week, then say so.

- Many people with learning disabilities are very affectionate and loving. They can be very demonstrative. Do not let this worry you. You will soon lose your inhibitions even if at first you feel embarrassed about this. For many clients a hug is their only way of communicating their liking for you.
- Expect normal standards of behaviour and you are most likely to receive them. You do your clients a disservice if you excuse bad manners too easily on the grounds of learning disability. Politeness and good manners can be learnt by clients and make them more socially acceptable.
- People with learning disabilities do not have a very long concentration span so do not be disheartened if a client only seems interested in one activity for a short time.
- Above all, remember that people with learning disabilities are individuals with their own personalities and likes and dislikes. You cannot be categorised and labelled and neither can a person with learning disabilities.

A music session should also be looked upon as an opportunity to relate musical/dance activities to other areas of life in an attempt to improve abilities such as socialisation, co-ordination and communication. Music has one tremendous advantage over speech in that it affects most people on a deep emotional level and through music some people, who had formerly chosen to remain silent, have been successfully encouraged to speak. It can also serve to slow down speech or to encourage quieter speech where necessary.

Approaching the group with the attitude that nothing is impossible is the most likely way to obtain positive results. Keeping an open mind and remaining flexible make it possible to take advantage of situations as they present themselves; for example, building on any spontaneous interest shown in a song or dance, allowing participants to change instrument when the mood takes them, or spending more time discussing a projected slide in response to someone's display of interest in a particular picture.

Through music we are striving to help people reach their full potential as individuals, at the same time enriching the quality of their lives to such an extent that they no longer think of themselves as 'people with learning disabilities'.

Finally, I hope that this book will provide guidance and encouragement to anyone interested in bringing music and related activities into the lives of people with learning disabilities.

Chapter 1
A SPECIAL MUSIC AREA

It may not be possible to have a specific room within the hospital set aside solely for music, as recommended by certain books, but this need not be a disadvantage. Indeed, some challenging behaviour groups do not benefit from leaving their unit to go to another unit. They appear to be more comfortable and secure in familiar surroundings rather than in unfamiliar ones and less likely to exhibit destructive or other anti-social behaviour in these conditions. Given that the leader of a music group will most likely have to make do with whatever area is available, the main criterion is to find somewhere with as little distraction as possible. Whether the group contains anti-social individuals or otherwise, it is always best to seek a place away from the mainstream of activity where the session is unlikely to be interrupted by passers-by curious to find out what is going on. The size of the room available will probably be determined by circumstances but, if at all possible, a large room serving as a thoroughfare should be avoided, while a small, more cosy, room restricts the number of people attending. A compromise is normally called for.

A room with windows looking out onto passing cars and people is distracting. It may be necessary to draw curtains to restrict the view to the outside. Maintaining the concentration of the group for a whole hour (the usual duration of a session) is difficult enough without outside activities drawing attention away from the music session. Having established that the music area is as free from distraction as it can be, there are other factors to consider, such as heating. Working in a room with an independent or adjustable heating system helps because most working environments tend to be overheated and as the heating of the rooms is generally linked, it can mean sessions taking place in sauna-like conditions. This often has the effect of sending the least active group members to sleep long before the end of the session.

Writing about heating may well appear unnecessary but stems from the experience and the frustration of watching participants in groups lose concentration due to their being too hot. As most people receive only one hour a week of music at the most, it is to everyone's advantage to create as comfortable an environment as possible.

Another consideration, if slides are to be projected during the sessions, is the quality of the curtains or blinds available as well as ensuring that there is a small table for the projector, preferably one light enough for one person to manage.

Bearing in mind that several members of the group may suffer from some visual impairment, it is vital, in order that everyone can benefit, that slides are shown in a properly blacked out room to prevent unclear misty images. If no satisfactory curtains are available, it is worth the effort of making some out of discarded black-out curtains or similar material.

Preparing the space for a music session can take time, especially if furniture and chairs need to be brought from other rooms. The session time is precious and, wherever possible, enlisting temporary help to set up the room prior to the beginning of a session is desirable.

The venue used for a music session can be made more inviting and cheery by decorating with relevant posters. The atmosphere of the music area will certainly be a contributory factor in determining how successful the sessions are and, given time and patience, a suitably conducive one can be established.

Chapter 2
THE GROUP

2.1 Structure

Whenever possible the size and structure of the group should be carefully planned. This means taking into consideration the abilities of participants, types of activities planned, general standards of behaviour and the amount of co-worker help available, as well as the number of sessions held per week. It is important to be flexible and to allow for mood swings and absences of co-workers and members who might not choose to attend the session each week, while maintaining a steady core of people which remains relatively unchanged from week to week. This will help to give the group a strong feeling of stability.

SIZE

Optimum working conditions would dictate that a large group of people should not attend a session together. However if, by limiting the numbers, those excluded are deprived of music, then it is difficult for the session leader to turn people away. Ultimately though, the size of the room and the type of client involved will influence any increases in attendance. For several months the numbers attending a session running in an occupational therapy unit fluctuated between 14 and 16. However, this was a well established group who behaved well and, though of mixed ability, mostly participated to a great extent. It had started out as a group of about eight, but as time went by more and more people in the unit asked to come along and numbers went up. The line had to be drawn when it became impossible to get any more chairs in the room and still close the door!

The group size hinges on two factors, namely how group members behave, and the amount of assistance available from co-workers. Initially the leader has to 'feel' his or her way around the group, to get to know the members just as they have to get to know the leader. A comfortable relaxed atmosphere can be expected to develop with time. People who exhibit anti-social behaviour will benefit from being in a small group, preferably with only one or two others in addition to the leader. It is also to the definite advantage of those displaying anti-social behaviour to be able to receive undivided attention once in a while. In the case of Maria and Julie, both of whom exhibited anti-social behaviour on occasion, they seemed to open up far more when seen separately. This was particularly evident with Julie who tended to mime words when speaking or singing and had to be encouraged to make herself heard. When I was able to see her for part of a session on her own she mimed far less. The reason could have been that in the presence of Maria, who sang and spoke well, Julie took a back seat and let Maria do most of the work. Whether this was to avoid competition, or just laziness, is hard to know. Suffice it to say that Julie definitely benefited from having time alone with the session leader every so often.

Bearing in mind that one aim of the sessions is to encourage socialisation and communication between group members, it is better to keep the numbers of people in the more difficult groups to two or three at the most. Activities such as dancing demand a minimum number of people, while projects such as plays and concerts require at least six people.

A large group has the advantage that group activities such as plays can be carried out with ease. Participation and the pleasure gained by performing in front of a large group are greater than with a small group. In a large group the range of individual abilities is often considerable and this in itself leads to increased participation, as the more able people usually help the less able. This can take the form of handing out an instrument, placing it correctly in another's hands, and showing how to play it.

The main aim is to create a stable, relaxed and balanced group. If certain personalities disrupt the atmosphere it is better if they are removed rather than allowing the group to suffer as a whole. Often such individuals calm down once they realise that disruptive behaviour leads to exclusion from the session. In groups whose members generally behave well, such disruptive behaviour tends to be rare and, when it does occur, is due to the 'culprit' being rather out of sorts that day.

UNPREDICTABLE OR DISRUPTIVE PARTICIPANTS

A group consisting of unpredictable or disruptive members functions best when numbers are kept low, perhaps between two and four. If dealing with such individuals, even if as few as two or three, it would be wise for the leader to enrol some assistance to begin with until confident enough to cope alone with any eventualities. People who can be unpredictable will need to be monitored by co-workers used to their behaviour, at least until the leader and members become used to each other. The structure of the group will be particularly important in this type of group. The presence of two individuals who do not get on can completely unbalance a whole group in which case a solution could be attendance at separate sessions where they do not have to tolerate each other's presence.

People's moods vary from week to week and they may be able to tolerate other people in the group on odd occasions. However, consistency and continuity are two key words when running a happy, well-balanced session, and number fluctuations from week to week are to be avoided. It is better to decide on who to include in a group and to vary the number as little as possible, although this format applies most of all when dealing with unpredictable personalities. In the normal course of events, when no-one is a danger to themselves or anyone else, the more the merrier!

Concerning exclusion of certain individuals, another category of person one might not wish to include in a group is the sort who, while being very enthusiastic, makes loud or continuous noises throughout the session. This tries everyone's patience and leads to frayed nerves and cross words directed towards the source of the noise. As well as noisy or very disruptive people, someone constantly demanding attention from the group leader, and who continues to do so despite gentle persuasion to refrain, could be seen on their own, but definitely not within a group where harmony is being actively promoted!

VARYING ABILITIES

Another point to consider when structuring a group is the range of the abilities of the members. Profoundly physically disabled people benefit more from being in a group of their own, with a great deal of assistance on hand. However, much depends on the type of disability and there is no reason not to include people who have difficulty walking, or may be wheel-chair bound, but are able to use their hands, with an otherwise physically able group. Such members can join in with instrument playing and singing and do not require special attention as a result of their disability. It is also surprising to what extent people who have problems with co-ordination are able to participate in activities like dancing.

Some people with learning disabilities suffer from an impaired capacity for selective attention to sounds. In some cases this faculty is completely absent and all sounds reach them unselectively. For instance they may be unable to ignore background noise to follow a conversation. This malfunction means that, like the hard of hearing, their potential for communication is reduced.

Regarding the degree of learning disability present among the group members, it is probably best to include anyone at all who expresses a desire to attend the session. A wide spectrum of abilities has the advantage that not only do the more able tend to look after and encourage the less able, but the less able seem to try harder to sing or dance etc. when they see what it is possible to achieve. No feeling of competition is engendered in a session and everyone is made to feel they have achieved something. Leaders should ensure that after every performance, be it a song, dance, etc., a performer is always clapped and cheered regardless of the 'standard' of performance reached.

SEATING

The seating arrangement is another important factor. To some extent it depends on the activities planned for any particular session. The following examples from my experience illustrate this. When I showed slides I placed the projector on a small table in the middle of the group and we all positioned ourselves so that we could see the screen at one end of the room. When we were playing music and singing, however, we tended to sit in a horse-shoe/circle shape, leaving a space at one end where people could stand while they performed. It was a good shape to sit in as we were all facing one another and it left space in the middle for individuals to perform a dance on their own, should they so wish. I made a point of trying to fit myself into the horse-shoe shape as much as possible in an attempt to blend in more as a participant than a 'leader' and hence to put more onus on group members to initiate songs and dances etc. without prompting from me. Often if there was a spare seat, vacated by a performer, I would move temporarily into this seat and, in so doing, be able to give some encouragement or help to some of the less able people.

2.2 Roles within the group

Maintaining a routine within a group is essential so long as it does not involve too much repetition. Certain participants adopt particular roles and/or behaviours which they adhere to rigidly from week to week. For instance these might comprise always sitting in the same position within the group, sitting next to certain people, or being the person, or one of the people, to hand the instruments round.

Members may take it on themselves to perform a certain activity or, having been asked once, will see it as their 'job' in future sessions. Cathy was one such person who handed the instruments out and remembered faithfully who played which instrument from session to session. She was also the one to accompany Brenda (who was blind) to the toilet and woe betide anyone who tried to take over either of these jobs! Cathy would be most put out if she felt that her position was being usurped. Other roles might include carrying the leader's instruments to the car at the end of a session, putting away the group's own instruments, tidying chairs, seeing some people back to their different areas within the unit etc.

To begin with, it is on the whole easier to allow the group to settle into the roles they feel most comfortable with. However, once music sessions have become established as a regular and routine part of everyone's lives, new roles can be introduced. Depending on individual personalities, some people could be encouraged to try out different activities. The ease with which this may be achieved depends very much on how 'safe' people feel with the activity they have chosen. If, for example, someone comes from a situation where each and every day for many years was spent making dish cloths, they might naturally tend to be less adventurous than otherwise. But in each of us there exists the capacity for change. Encouragement, accompanied by gentle persuasion, can often lead to experimenting with new activities and to gaining new experiences.

2.3 Communication between members

Over and above any socialising factor, whereby people who may normally meet infrequently have an opportunity to mix socially, the music session provides a unique situation for participants to relax and concentrate on making music. As singing tends to encourage some people to speak more, communication between group members is increased during a session. This may take the form of someone showing another how to hold and play an instrument while explaining how to do so. Or it may involve a participant asking someone to sing a song with them.

Regular use of name songs should ensure early on that the group know each others' names, that is, for those who are capable of recognising people, learning names, and are able to match names to faces. It is actually the case that even people with profound   learning disabilities fall into this category. The following name game can be repeated at the beginning of each session for a few weeks. A light musical instrument such as a bunch of bells is tossed by one person to another who speaks his or her name when catching the bells. This process is repeated until everyone in the group has been tossed the bells and said their name.

As one of the intentions is to encourage participation between group members, verbal interaction between individuals is always to be encouraged. (The use of music to help improve levels of communication displayed by individuals is covered more fully in Chapter 6.) However, an exception would be someone striking up a loud conversation while another person is in the process of singing. A few gentle words to point out that someone else is performing, and that everyone is listening, usually does the trick.

It is a good idea to try to divert the general conversation away from the leader. While I always tried to include everyone in my groups in my life as a whole, by telling them where I was going on holiday, when I was moving house, how the dog was, etc., I felt it was important that they should communicate more with each other rather than just with me. As I was attempting to create an atmosphere where everyone felt on an equal footing with each other, with equal capabilities, it was important that I was not seen as the only person in the group with anything important to say. As everyone in my group got to know each other better, the atmosphere became very relaxed and there were times when the sessions actually started without me! The instruments would have been given out, those who had difficulty seeing and/or walking would have been led to their seats and settled down, and one of the more able singers would have led everyone into a good 'joining in' song.

What is impressive about this turn of events, is that some group members now had the confidence to initiate singing on their own and to communicate what they were going to sing, in advance, to the others. Years of experience have shown that singing together in a group situation definitely increases the degree of communication displayed by individual group members towards one another. Music really does help to break down barriers.

2.4 Coping with Mood Changes

Like everyone else, people with   learning disabilities are subject to mood swings or changes in temperament. People without   learning disabilities disguise these changes fairly easily. Sudden outbursts of temper or other displays of emotion are not generally tolerated in a typical work situation; indeed, one notable sign of maturity in 'normal' people is the ability to hide feelings and carry on as usual, regardless of how they may be feeling inside (not always advantageous as it can be detrimental to health or, on occasion, lead to breakdowns). People with   learning disabilities do not generally suffer from such repression of feeling and tend to be very open and matter of fact generally. In fact, one of their many loveable facets is their ability to voice feelings and express themselves with little or no inhibition.

It is pointless trying to play a part with them, or present a certain image. Any such façade will be ignored as they are only interested in the real person behind. It is one of the joys of working with people with learning disabilities that one can be oneself and interact on a more relaxed and natural level than usual.

However, the inability to control feelings can have drawbacks as any change in mood is generally immediately obvious. The smallest of things can have seemingly disproportionate impact, causing great joy or conversely misery. It is not uncommon for a leader returning to a group after a momentary absence (to bring in extra chairs for example) to find a participant in tears and quite distressed. When investigated, the cause of the upset usually turns out to be along the lines of 'so-and-so looked at me in a funny way' or something to that effect. I tended to deal with such situations in the following manner.

I would try to calm things down by defusing the situation and explaining to the 'offended' person that the 'offender' did not really mean to 'look in a certain way', or say whatever he/she had said, while following this with back-up from the 'offender' that indeed they had not meant it at all and it was all a misunderstanding. This approach generally restored the peace pretty quickly, but for those times when it failed to work, I would escort the upset person back to their section on the unit so that they could calm down in their own time.

This approach was used for a large occupational therapy group; with a 'disturbed' group it would hardly have been appropriate as sudden mood swings can be extremely dramatic, being generally unpredictable and often violent in nature. A quiet word would hardly do the trick here. Assistance is essential and individuals who become destructive (for example hurling instruments across the room) have to be restrained from hurting their neighbours or from causing further damage. This can be successfully done by sitting with them and gently holding their hands. Attempts can then be made to calm them by drawing their attention once more to the music and encouraging them to sing. If the violent behaviour is directed towards themselves, the same procedure is recommended.

Occasionally, an apparently calm person might turn and hit their neighbour either with their hand or instrument. Such behaviour nearly always calls for removal from the music area. The all-male challenging behaviour session that I ran, had the advantage of a secure garden area with seats and swings where disruptive people could be allowed to wander until they appeared to have calmed down sufficiently to be allowed to return inside, back to the session. By using different types of music, playing different instruments and using different rhythms, it was possible to influence the group mood for the better.

Being able to cope with mood changes requires:

1. being aware that these can, and do, take place with alarming rapidity
2. being aware that they can often be followed by a complete reversal to the previous state of behaviour
3. knowing what course of action is best in the circumstances
4. being flexible and coping with each situation as it arises, with both compassion and understanding.

Chapter 3
RELATIONSHIP WITH CO-WORKERS

3.1 Co-worker–therapist liaison

A good relationship between co-workers and therapist benefits everyone. It goes without saying that co-workers spend many hours, most days of every week, with clients, while the leader of a music session only sees them for a few hours a week at the most. It is, therefore, imperative to discover as much relevant information as possible about the group members, through valuing the viewpoints and knowledge held by the co-workers who have regular contact with them. Co-workers can see the extent of response, if any, to a session. A group member sitting apparently completely lifeless and who makes no effort to play or even hold the musical instrument placed on his/her knees, may appear to the leader to be gaining nothing whatsoever from the session. However, if that person's normal behaviour is to wander round the room shouting aimlessly at the top of their voice, then the music would indeed appear to be having some influence on behaviour. Only by talking with the co-workers can one discover the customary behaviour for any of the individuals taking part and, as a result, determine what effect the music is having. Co-workers can also provide the therapist with much valuable information concerning the abilities and/or personalities of people participating in the music sessions.

Another consideration not to overlook is that co-workers must not feel usurped in any way in their endeavour to improve the quality of life of the clients. They deal with day-to-day routine matters and often bear the brunt of any frustrations experienced by some clients. Some of these frustrations sometimes culminate in actual physical attacks on co-workers. Caring for clients on a daily basis can be a fairly arduous and thankless task and it can understandably be somewhat galling for co-workers to witness a normally difficult client leaping to their feet with evident glee, muttering 'music! music!' as they rush towards the music session room. Any break in routine tends to result in a display of enthusiasm by clients just because it is precisely that: a break in routine. What is more, a music session tends to be an enjoyable affair, involving different activities and a chance to participate in a group activity, and it happens only once a week, all of which lends it a novelty value denied to other daily activities. Understandably there must be times when it is vexing to see the music therapist themselves being treated with greater respect and affection than some of the co-workers who spend most of their waking day trying to help clients and generally improve the quality of their lives.

It is important that these facts are borne in mind when interacting with co-workers at the venues where the music sessions are held. Co-workers deserve respect and consideration and, whenever it is helpful, the therapist will make it a habit to offer feedback regarding any changes/achievements witnessed at the music sessions. During the rest of the week co-workers might then use this to develop achievements/talents displayed by clients, and thus further improve their quality of life. These activities might take the following form:

1. Encourage reading the words of choruses by practising singing the choruses during the day.
2. Taking ten minutes each day to practise simple dance steps to imprint them in the group's memory so that they are less likely to be forgotten by the time of the next music session.
3. Playing a cassette of songs sung by clients and recorded during a music session. This could be done during other activities such as handicrafts.
4. Playing particular types of music for specific individuals can help change their mood. Certain passages of music have a calming effect on agitated people, conversely, other pieces can stimulate ordinarily inactive people. This can be used to good effect in everyday life.

A good relationship between co-workers and therapist does indeed enhance the lives of everyone concerned.

3.2 Assistance

With some groups it is vital to have some assistance, at least during the initial stages. The extent to which assistance is needed depends upon the type and number of people within a group. Potentially violent or unpredictable people, that is those who display challenging behaviour, will of necessity require some supervision during a session. It is impossible to simultaneously attempt to lead a session, play an instrument, try to protect instruments temporarily not used, and fend off undesirable behaviour. In music sessions with people with   learning disabilities it is very rare though that any musical instruments come to grief and if it happens is likely to be caused by misadventure rather than intent.

With one particularly disturbed group, two co-workers attended the sessions for several weeks until I had become acquainted with the clients (three in this particular group) and they, in turn, had become used to me. Becoming familiarised with group members, and they in turn with the leader, is essential before anything much can be achieved during a music session. The length of time this takes depends on the personalities involved, the number within the group and the number of distractions which abound.

Assistance is also extremely valuable when the group members are poorly motivated or physically unable to hold an instument and need help, or when sheer numbers makes it necessary. On occasion, students training at the hospital would visit my sessions on the occupational therapy unit and their presence invariably contributed a great deal, both in terms of encouraging the clients and also by providing an audience in front of which the clients could show off their musical/dance abilities.

Chapter 4
THE SESSION

4.1 How to structure the session

Once a group has been satisfactorily established, keeping a record of how different people respond is a good idea. A chart which suggests ways of keeping such a record is provided in *Music for Living* by Miriam Wood (1982). It is stating the obvious to say that everyone responds differently to music and this must always be borne in mind when attempting to assess an individual's response to music.

Care must also be taken never to underestimate people's abilities. It is all too easy to assume that because a person appears to be very poorly co-ordinated, suffers from visual impairment and possibly a speech impediment too, that he or she will only be capable of playing the maracas. It is an easy mistake to make which may come to light at a later date when the person in question shows enough dexterity to cope fairly well with a xylophone and indeed derives great pleasure from doing so.

Mistakes are sometimes made because no-one is aware of the capabilities of each participant, particularly if it is their first time at a music session or first opportunity to play a musical instrument. If this is the case with some or all group members, perseverance through trial and error is the best policy to find out what everyone is capable of and which instrument they prefer to play, given a choice.

The emphasis here lies in the phrase 'given a choice' as instruments are sometimes handed out ad hoc either by the leader of the session, or by a group member who has elected to be in charge of handing out the instruments to those who perhaps might not or cannot attempt to get them for themselves. Talking to participants individually and allowing the opportunity and time to look in the boxes will help them find an instrument they would like to play. Handing out different instruments from week to week to those unable to do this is a chance to see what they seem to prefer. Even if people have a favourite instrument it is always a good idea to offer them something new once in a while, providing of course that they are not upset by the change.

Most people value some sort of routine to provide a firm base to work from and people with learning disabilities value structure within their lives too. Remembering that this structure is mostly beyond their control, when they are therefore able to create some form of routine it brings some added security to their lives. A routine can be built into the music sessions by following a roughly similar theme for the starting activity and the finishing activity. The procedure I tended to use in my sessions is as follows:

We nearly always started with a strongly rhythmic tune (Breton, Irish, Scandinavian etc.). I played it on the Appalachian dulcimer as this is a fairly loud instrument with which it is possible to establish a good rhythm. Everyone joined in, using various percussion instruments and wildly differing rhythms and volume levels. The advantages of starting like this are two-fold. First, it requires everyone to join in, so immediately you have participation, and secondly it helps to put everyone in a happier frame of mind and establish that they are now in a music session where the main theme is enjoyment.

Our finishing activity consisted of everyone joining in with the favourite song of the moment, determined as a result of requests from the group, and led by me playing an instrument. I played an instrument solely because I found that it encouraged the group as a whole to participate, a few tending to falter if I stopped playing.

Other routines will be established by people in the group acting of their own volition, and include activities already mentioned such as handing out the instruments, sitting in a certain position within the group, carrying a particular instrument out to the car etc. Some of these activities may serve to give the person concerned an increased feeling of worth and self-importance.

Establishing long-term projects gives the group something to aim for, and organising 'parties' provides something to look forward to. We held a 'party' roughly once a month which usually consisted of a packet of biscuits, which ran to two each with luck, and occasionally orange juice in the summer. Parties were always announced well in advance and sometimes arranged to coincide with forthcoming events, for example, certain people returning from their holidays. Having this little treat at regular intervals appeared to make these sessions a little bit special and, hopefully, more of a social occasion to be enjoyed.

4.2 Tailoring activities for individual needs

As well as encouraging people to practice activities (songs, dances, etc.) that they are good at, paradoxically it is also important to link musical activities to activities that they are not good at. How this is done depends on the particular weakness in question, and discussion with someone with expertise in physiotherapy might help to generate ideas. For example, Adrian, who suffered from poor physical co-ordination and visual impairment benefited by using particular instruments to help his co-ordination. Having a wide variety of instruments at one's disposal is essential, as some require two hands, some fine, definite movement, others a shaking action, and so on. Judicial selection of instrument(s) may bring about improvement in time (but results overnight are unlikely!).

It is effective to link musical activities to other interests of the group members. For example, Philip belonged to a rather disturbed all-male group and did not speak as coherently as he could although he was very fluent when amongst people he knew. However Philip had an obsession with buses, so much so that whenever he saw a vehicle resembling a bus he shouted 'Bus! Bus!' repeatedly. During one night that the clients' minibus had been parked outside his room, Philip kept everyone awake by standing by the window pointing outside and shouting 'Bus!'. There was no doubt about Philip's passion, and a song was written with him in mind. This song had the dual function of using the word 'bus' many times, to attract Philip's attention, and also incorporated the names of different group members in the chorus to involve them as well. The song was a great success and was regularly used with other groups from then on.

The complete words and music can be found in the centre pull-out supplement.

Music makes a difference

A Practical Guide

to developing music sessions with people with learning disabilities

Toni Bunnell

A selection of songs

Published by M&K Update Ltd

Going on the Bus

Words & music by Toni Bunnell © 1987

Chorus
>Here comes Philip, he's going on the bus
>Going on the bus, going on the bus
>Here comes Philip, he's going on the bus
>Going on the bus today.

Verses
>The bus goes fast, the bus goes slow
>Along the street, there's three in a row
>Never when you want them, when it's pouring down
>You never see a bus alone, always in a crowd.

>Some are red and some are blue
>Some are coloured in almost every hue
>But a bus is a bus when all is said and done
>Quicker than walking and much more fun.

>So you wait there for hours in the hope that one will come
>Then when you've given up and started to run
>One comes along right out of the blue
>No time to reach the next stop, you may as well go home.

>Under bridges, up hills and down
>Through the countryside and into the town
>Down by the river, the journey nearly done
>The last bus creeps home with the setting of the sun.

The Magic Ring

Words & music by Toni Bunnell © 1985

Take the cand - le,___ hold it way up high,___ let us
stand here to-ge-ther by the heat___ of the fire. Fill your glas- ses,___ drink them
down in one.___ Pull your cloaks hard a-round you 'till the night it is done.

Chorus

Don't go chang- ing,___ don't go chang- ing,___ don't go

1. chang - ing a - ny more.

2. Don't go more.

2. For there's magic and there's spells and all
To keep us here together when the darkness
   it does fall
And there's shadows and there's evil things
Waiting out there for us, just looking for the ring.

3. Lock the doors now, bar the windows fast
Huddle close together, lay your head down
   on the mat
But be careful, ere you fall asleep
And down through the chimney the thing
   it starts to creep.

4. For there was laughter when the sun shone high
And fun to be had out underneath the sky
But when the dusk came and the light grew dim
Swiftly inside came us all every one.

5. For the ring it must be guarded well
And held safely for us for who alone can tell
What would happen if it went from our midst
And the dark came upon us, never more to lift.

6. So leave the ring from off your finger
Let it rest easy now, let it in your pocket linger
For to wear it, just one more time
Means you vanish from sight and the ring they
   will find.

7. So go easy and go softly
Watch every corner, watch every nook and cranny
And remember, when the night it falls
Hold the ring closely to you and think of us all.

Sophie Emmeline

Words & music by Toni Bunnell © 1991

Oh, So - phie Em - me - line,___ to-day I plant - ed a tree.___ Oh,

So - phie Em - me - line,___ I wish you'd been there to see,___ And the sun shone

high a- bove,___ the___ wind blew hard thro' the trees,___ but most of

all, So-phie Em-me - line, I wish you'd been there with me.

2. Today the birds are on the wing, I hear them calling as they fly
As generations have done before, they sing again for you and I
For many years have been and gone since you last trod this earth
And I think of you now, Sophie Emmeline, and all the years since your birth.

3. The graveyard sank into decline, no-one came to tend the weeds
The climbing ivy covered the ground, the roses went to seed
You slept alone then, Sophie Emmeline, no hand nor foot came near you
The weeds advanced ever onwards, hid the headstones from view.

4. But things are changing, Sophie Emmeline, trees are growing here and there
Planted now, Sophie Emmeline, with love and with care
And as they grow up towards the sky, they'll cast their shadows on the ground
No more light for the weeds to grow, the headstones once more will be found.

5. Oak and ash again will grow between the gravestones like yours
Towering high above the ground, protecting you from all harm
And I've packed my oak tree firm in the ground, but as I turn to go
I think of you, Sophie Emmeline, who lived so many years ago.

6. And as the weeks and months come and go the trees will bring with them new life
A promise and hope of things to come, a turning point in our lives
And you will always be there, Sophie Emmeline, in my thoughts for evermore
Besides my oak tree here in the ground, a piece of England now secure.

Repeat verse one.

You of the Dark Night

Words & music by Toni Bunnell © 1985

Oh the day is past wait-ing and the night it has come And the stars they shine down once a-gain___ On you of the dark night who car-ries the bright light In search of those lost from the vale.___ For you are the lead-er, we fol-low you now,___ we stum-ble on long aft-er dark it has come.___ We va-lue your wis-dom, we trea-sure your smile,___ we look to___ you now as our guide.___

You came to our village
We know not where from
In your long flowing clothes you stood there
And your look held us spellbound
With the warmth it gave out
You brought magic indeed to the air
And the flowers they grew taller, just look at them now
They ramble all over the gardens about
'Tis long since that creatures ran lame in this place
And long since the rivers ran high.

For you brought with you magic
And you taught us the ways
Lost long ago from our lives
Of how to cure illness
With herbs from the hedge
And how to heal aches with our hands
And we listened to all that you had to say
Gathered it up in our minds straight away
Learned how to know when the North wind would blow
And when to put plough to the soil.

And when the moon rose
To be full in the sky
We joined all our hands one by one
And stood there in silence
While the magic it grew
And the clouds they moved over the sun.
For you are the daughter of sunrise and light
You move with the flowers and dance with the breeze
And our lives they are swept with a fire so bright
Like the wind that moves fast through the trees.

And as we search now
For those lost on the fell
No doubt it lies deep in our thoughts
Only the faith in our
Queen of the night
Who carries her love like a sword
And soon we will find them and carry them home
The children so lost to us now
And gather them to us around the fireside
To hear once again tales of old.

The Dead Man's Hand

Words & music by Toni Bunnell © 1974

The rob-ber counts the sto-len jewels when the night is done.

The ev-il hand shone no more, now the day had come.

He took the hand out of his bag and thanked it with a sigh.

This hand would prove his for-tune yet, with its cand-le burn-ing high.

Chorus

And all a-long the al-ley way where the dev-il lurks,

The dead man's hand holds the cand-le while the rob-ber works.

Taken from the gallows on Sunday e'en at dark
When all the trees on the skyline looked evil, black and stark
The hand was from a highwayman who rode the lanes at dusk
'Till late one night he was captured: he'd taken his final risk.

He was taken to the gallows high up on Devil's Hill
Where people came from round about and each one wished him ill
Had he not taken from the rich each night when it grew dark
And now he'd suffer for his crimes, they'd put an end to this lark.

The dead man's hand with the candle served as a magic charm
'Twas enough to give all the rich folk much cause for alarm;
With its dim and steady flame glowing through the night
All those who lay a-bed would surely then sleep tight.

If ever that evil flame wavered or died
To linger was but foolish and away the robber shied
He took warning from the flame that all was not well
Someone in the house had stirred and broken his magic spell.

But while he spoke the magic words softly in the calm
The burning candle in the hand would keep him safe from harm.
"Sleep all who sleep, wake all who wake,
But be as dead for the dead man's sake."

Ride Your Horses

Words & music by Toni Bunnell © 1982

Chorus

Ride your hor-ses through the night, ride them fast, your time to keep. Come ride your hor-ses through the night when all a-round lies still in sleep.

Verse 1

And as you ride a-long the lanes, hard a-gainst the driv-ing rain, don't spare the horse, keep rid-ing, do. The mail at all costs must get through.

2. The clock chimes one, you hear it now
Ringing from some nearby town
Where people dream all in their sleep
No thought for you with your time to keep.
CHORUS

3. And as the horse it clatters on
You think of lurking highwaymen
Who lie in wait no-one knows where
Hoping to trap you in their snare.
CHORUS

4. Three miles to London shows the stone
Not long now until you're home
With messages from distant parts
To help pay debts and lighten hearts.
CHORUS

5. And now you're at your journey's end
Through the courtyard, round the bend
On towards the hanging lights
That welcome strangers from the night.
CHORUS

6. And no-one knows who rode the lanes
No-one thanks you for your pains
But tonight, once more, the mail got through
Thanks to a rider, one of the few.
CHORUS

Hang on the Ledge

Words & music by Toni Bunnell © 1984

Chorus

Hang on the ledge, boy, hang on the ledge We're co-ming up for you

slow - ly Hang on the ledge, boy, hang on the ledge

Keep your-self straight now, try not to break now And just hang on the ledge.

Chorus
Hang on the ledge, boy, hang on the ledge
We're coming up for you slowly
Hang on the ledge, boy, hang on the ledge
Keep yourself straight now, try not to break now
And just hang on the ledge.

Verses
1. You're such a small boy, as small as they come
   Not the sort to get stuck at the first bend.
   But small as you are, you mean all to me
   You who climb chimneys, like others climb trees
   For after all you are my son.

2. 'Tis many a time thro' years gone by
   I've cursed these long, high chimneys
   That caused the death of many a lad
   Who'd sit on high and sing and shout
   But 'twas rare we got them out.

3. For the chimneys they do twist and turn
   Not built for human bodies
   To crawl along them up and down
   With brush in hand and sweating brow
   All for the master.

4. The masters of the houses great
   Care little for the chimney sweep
   They care not if he lives or dies
   Or where indeed his body lies
   Save that their fire burns bright.

5. These little boys as black as coal
   They walk with crooked backs now
   And do their best to earn their keep
   Forever tossing in their sleep
   In fear of the dark.

6. So think back on these little ghosts
   Of chimney sweeps from long ago
   Who braved the hot and winding bends
   Of tunnels that would never end
   Brave little boys indeed.

Chapter 5
THE MUSIC

Music has been proven to be of great value when incorporated into the everyday lives of people with learning disabilities and a number of books have been published on the subject. Although some would disagree, viewing music as merely a harmless but pleasant way of passing the time, evidence now overwhelmingly points to more far-reaching effects and advantages.

5.1 Types of Music

The type of music to use/play during music sessions depends very much on personal taste. Like the use of rhythm however, it is important to be aware of the possible effects of different types of music prior to starting sessions. As with different rhythms, certain types of music promote a calm and peaceful atmosphere, while others may incite aggressive behaviour. The type of music chosen depends very much on the personality types of the group members and what it is hoped to achieve during the sessions.

Before proceeding any further it is important to be clear what the music is for and who it is intended for. The following list outlines some points for consideration:

What is the music for?
- listening
- rhythmic exercises
- singing
- dancing
- special theme (e.g. Christmas)

Who is the music intended for?
- what is the size of the group?
- what is the level of abilities?
- what is the age range?
- what are their interests?
- what disabilities occur in the group?

The mood of individual group members and/or the group as a whole, can be influenced through the careful selection of instruments, rhythm and different types of music. Being able to play several instruments helps to provide variety and enables live rather than taped music to be used. However, the inability to play an instrument should not deter would-be enthusiasts, particularly as it is possible to learn an instrument, such as a guitar, as the sessions progress. Meantime, well-selected taped music, used with consideration at certain points during a session, will be invaluable. It has the virtue of allowing the leader, particularly if working alone, to actively participate in the session and to encourage group members when playing their instrument or in whatever activity they are engaged in at the time.

5.2 The Instruments

LEADER'S INSTRUMENT
When choosing instruments to be played by the leader of a group, it is probably best to go for whichever

appeals the most. It is much easier to learn an instrument one is enthusiastic about, rather than selecting it because it is perceived as a good one to learn. The guitar is probably the most universal instrument played, being fairly versatile and easily transportable. The dulcimer is another good choice. Loud instruments like some brass ones would not perhaps be very wise as they tend to dominate a session and drown out the efforts of the group members. The piano, while useful, is somewhat limited in its ability to strike up a 'good' atmosphere (although this is obviously a matter of opinion) and has restrictions in that the session must go to the piano rather than the piano to the session. It is worth repeating that the best instrument for the leader is one which is familiar and which does not require too much concentration, thus enabling the leader to give maximum attention to the group, rather than struggling to play the instrument.

The instruments most familiar to the author and used in numerous sessions were the dulcimer, the harmonium, the fiddle, the guitar and the hurdy gurdy. The dulcimer was found to be the most versatile. This dulcimer was of the Appalachian variety, laid flat across the knees and played by placing the fingers of the left hand in the necessary positions on the fret or finger board (fretting), while the right hand struck out the tune directly with the fingers or with a plectrum.

The dulcimer is one of the simplest instruments to learn as it can be tuned to an open tuning, meaning that even without any fingers on the fret board, a pleasant sound can still be produced. In a word, it is virtually impossible to play anything discordant. It is an ideal instrument for a non-musician to learn in a relatively short time. The guitar, by comparison, needs hard work to learn chords before anything musical can be achieved.

At the time of writing, cheap dulcimers were obtainable in some city music shops for about £150. Care must be taken to ensure that the instrument has been fretted properly, in order that it will play in tune. A reasonable dulcimer can be bought for £250 and upwards at craft fairs and folk festivals throughout the country or directly from instrument makers advertising in folk magazines or through contacts at local folk clubs.

A word of caution for anyone buying an instrument such as a guitar or a dulcimer: it is well worth investing in a humidifier to control the humidity in the atmosphere surrounding the instrument in its case. In centrally-heated accommodation, this is a must.

Another reason the dulcimer lends itself particularly well to music sessions is that it is an extremely rhythmic instrument. It is excellent for striking out tunes with catchy rhythms and hence creates a vibrant atmosphere from the very start. It is strident, produces a fairly loud sound if required, and is louder than most other string instruments. This was illustrated by a group of roughly sixteen playing percussion instruments as loud as they could and who yet all came to a halt very soon after the leader's dulcimer ceased playing. As they had been intent on watching their instruments, the only way they could have known that the dulcimer had stopped was through hearing.

Most people are familiar with the guitar and its scope. Good instruments can be purchased easily and fairly cheaply, and plenty of guitar tutors are available for the learner.

The portable harmonium or pedal organ may seem a surprising choice for the leader but offers quite definite advantages. It can be set up in no time and played even in the absence of an electricity supply. It has a familiar piano-like keyboard and produces a very satisfying sound, though care must be taken to make sure songs do not come to sound too hymn-like! In recent years this has been superseded by the electronic keyboard. My harmonium has two sets of reeds and a knee swell which ensured that the second bank of reeds (an octave higher than the first) could be heard, hence resulting in an increase in volume of the sound produced. I used the harmonium a great deal in earlier sessions and more sparingly later as I started to play other instruments.

The fiddle is useful for playing tunes for dances. Short dances, lasting for two or three tunes, were very popular. Those who wanted to took to the floor, either on their own or with a partner, to dance in various different styles! They then returned to their seats to rest while I played something on my own. Though the fiddle is a good instrument for dances, a taped recording can easily be substituted and will serve the same purpose.

The hurdy gurdy produces a sound reminiscent of pipes at its best, or a terrible grating sound at its worst. However it is not an easy instrument to play and, unless prepared to put in hours and hours of practice, it is not worth pursuing.

THE GROUP'S INSTRUMENTS

When providing instruments for the group to use, the accent ought to be on balance of sound, variety of instruments, easy availability and the freedom to choose. However, the selection largely depends on what is available at the centre where the sessions are held. Once a good supply of instruments has been assembled it is important to make sure that everyone has the opportunity to try out different instruments. Some may prefer to have the same one week after week, while others welcome the chance to change from time to time. The choice, on occasion, could be prompted to improve co-ordination for example, but though a particular choice may be encouraged, it must never be enforced. The only type of instrument actively discouraged in the normal course of events is a very loud one such as a whistle. Apart from getting on everyone's nerves, the sound will undesirably dominate the group.

Provision of instruments has improved and a range of percussion instruments such as maracas, tambourines, castanets, drums, finger cymbals etc., will benefit the group. Depending on the ability of group members, additional instruments such as cheap or second-hand guitars or fiddles could be purchased. Surprising results can come about by giving someone the opportunity to try something out. I often allowed selected people in my groups to play my own instruments, in particular, the harmonium, dulcimer and fiddle. One person showed quite an aptitude for the fiddle and was able to hold it in roughly the right position and knock out a rough tune.

For some physically disabled people, items such as bells attached to a leather band which fastens round a wrist or ankle, are ideal as the slightest of movements is sufficient to produce sound.

For anyone hoping to start a music session without initial funding, it is possible to purchase instruments such as maracas, tambourines, bongo drums, etc., quite cheaply from music shops. Alternatively, jumble sales and second-hand shops often turn up the odd instrument at low cost. Provided they aren't in need of expensive repairs, and provided the price is not too high, they are worth buying. Schools and similar establishments occasionally have second-hand instruments they would be prepared to sell cheaply, something which is worth investigating.

HOME-MADE INSTRUMENTS

If no money is available at all, it is possible to make instruments from household odds and ends. There follows some ideas for home-made instruments.

Beaters

It is essential to experiment a bit to find the best head for beaters of any percussion instruments they are intended for. Possible materials are: metal (large nail), wood, rubber (small cheap balls), cork, foam (wound round tightly), pastry brushes.

Drums

There are two basic types of drum:
1   solid e.g. large tin, cardboard drum, wooden box
2   skin stretched over a base. Potential bases can be made using any tube e.g. drainpipe, cardboard, tin, plastic dustbin. The principle is to stretch the skin tightly over the top using strong sticky tape or lacing. Using rubber for the top is ideal but thick paper or plastic last quite well.
Resonance and tone depend on size, materials and type of beater. It is possible to make tuned sets or a pair (low and high) to play with the fingers like bongos.

Tambourines and Snare Drums

These are basically drums with jinglers or wires attached.

Claves

The sound is produced by banging two lengths of dowelling together. Length makes little difference to tone but thickness and type of wood do.

Clappers

Two flat bits of wood hinged together constitute this simple instrument.

Sand-blocks

Two blocks of wood covered each with a piece of sandpaper (using drawing pins to secure it). Different grades of sandpaper vary the tone when the blocks are rubbed against each other.

Shakers

Shakers consist of sealed cylinders which, though similar in appearance, produce a variety of sounds and volume when a selection of materials are used for the containers and these are filled with contents of different coarseness, e.g. dried peas, rice, sand.

Thunder-sheet

Sheet metal, for example the kind used for welding car body-work, makes interesting noises when waved. Care is needed to ensure sharp edges are well sanded down or covered with thick plastic tape to prevent mishaps.

Tea-chest Bass *fig 5.1*

A thick string such as washing line or sash cord is passed through a small hole drilled in the centre of the upturned base of a tea-chest (a large knot or tying the end of the cord to a small stick prevents it from slipping out). The cord's loose end is now tied firmly to the top of a broom handle. The bottom of the broom handle rests on a corner of the box and the string is plucked much like that of a double bass. Tone varies as the string tension is altered or the sound can be shortened by stopping the string. Gloves are recommended for sustained playing!

Gongs

Some types of hub caps make lovely gongs as do some metal tea-trays but others are awful! Gongs should be suspended from two strings attached to holes drilled in the edge and tied onto a frame or a short pole.

Scrapers

Any rough surfaces such as cheese graters, a flat strip of wood with grooves cut out or with strips tacked on, or wash boards, will all make simple instruments to play with metal thimbles or a stick.

fig 5.1

Chimes

Copper pipes used in plumbing make good chimes. Varying lengths and thicknesses give different very clearly-pitched notes. This instrument can be tuned exactly by measuring. For instance, a pipe twice as long as another and the same thickness rings an octave higher. The chimes are suspended by string passed through a pair of holes drilled in one end. Alternatively, it is easier to hit them, if both ends of the pipe have strings attached to a xylophone-type frame.

Xylophones *fig 5.2*

The essential principle for home-made xylophones is to select a set of items of the same type but of different sizes. Suitable materials include empty tins or flower pots, and milk bottles or mugs filled with different levels of water. Earthenware flower pots can either be hung up or placed on a plank and are played by hitting the side rather than the top. A more ambitious version involves a wooden frame to support keys, which can be made of wood, tile, slate or metal of varying lengths and/or thicknesses.

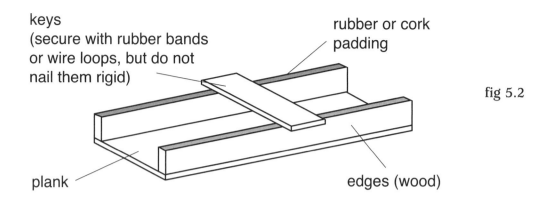

keys
(secure with rubber bands
or wire loops, but do not
nail them rigid)

rubber or cork
padding

fig 5.2

plank

edges (wood)

Other 'dirt-cheap' instruments

Balloons.

Kazoos (£4.00) from most music shops.

Jew's harps – not very easy to play though.

Bicycle bells (tune by adjusting the screws).

Mouth organs – plastic ones from about £4.

Old unwanted pianos can be adapted to create strange and interesting sounds by inserting items like corks, screws, paper, or wooden strips between or under the strings. Or else the action can be removed altogether to pluck like a harp.

Trumpet mouthpieces (from about £5) can be fitted to any sort of tube: hosepipe, bamboo pipe, copper pipe, and different notes obtained by altering the length of the tube with a plunger or by drilling holes in it.

5.3 Use of rhythm

The rhythm of the music played must be chosen with care. If something is known beforehand about the personalities of the people involved in a group, the session can be planned accordingly and the desired atmosphere developed. People who exhibit challenging behaviour tend to become calmer, less agitated and less aggressive if they listen to calm peaceful music. A slow, fairly quiet, repetitive rhythm can lull them into a more tranquil state. In contrast, a loud syncopated rhythm can rouse already agitated people and precipitate an outbreak of aggressive behaviour.

If however, the group members are normally fairly unresponsive and/or apathetic, then a loud syncopated rhythm can stir them into action. It might be worth purchasing a book on different rhythms and experimenting with them using a range of percussion instruments. Other in-depth music therapy books are also available (see bibliography).

In order to develop new and existing abilities it is recommended to make some form of regular assessment of the participants' skills. the table below shows one way this can be done.

EVALUATION FORM
CREATIVE ARTS THERAPIES

CLIENT   **SESSION LEADER**

Unit   Date   to

Client   ind.session   daily   1/2hr wkly   Art Therapy

is seen: group session   weekly   1hr wkly   Dance/Movement Therapy

                                                                Music Therapy

TOTAL HOURS of therapy per month   Conjunctive Therapy

A. RATING SCALE *circle one*   0 = none at all   1 = Low   2 = Average   3 = Good   4 = High

1. Degree of active involvement (physical)	0	1	2	3	4
2. Emotional involvement	0	1	2	3	4
3. Awareness of self	0	1	2	3	4
4. Ability to relate to others	0	1	2	3	4
5. Ability to relate to therapist	0	1	2	3	4
6. Orientation to surroundings	0	1	2	3	4
7. Perception of Reality	0	1	2	3	4
8. Toleration of closeness	0	1	2	3	4
9. Expression of appropriate effect	0	1	2	3	4
10. Expression of initiative	0	1	2	3	4
11. Engagement in creative process	0	1	2	3	4
12. Ability to integrate experience	0	1	2	3	4
13. Frustration tolerance	0	1	2	3	4

B. PROGRESS NOTES   Is this the initial evaluation on client?

C. COMMENTS (Treatment plans & goals; strengths & weaknesses; prognosis

6.1 Socialisation

Socialisation is an integral and important part of a music session. A regular session held in an occupational therapy department sometimes involved people from different areas coming together, that is, individuals who would not normally come into contact with each other on a daily basis. This session always involved participating in an activity together as a group and the group members grew to have a greater awareness of each other in a relaxed, enjoyable atmosphere.

Normally, people exhibiting challenging behaviour, and who might injure others, are kept separate from those not displaying these tendencies. However, within any group of people there will still be a range of personalities with varying degrees of sociability. Some might be withdrawn and show little inclination for joining in with activities and by judicious allocation of tasks and roles (mentioned in Chapter 3) it may be possible to draw such people out of themselves. As they become less withdrawn they are more likely to participate in the activities and more likely to socialise.

Group activities like dancing and long-term projects, such as preparing for and presenting a musical play or concert, assist greatly in encouraging socialisation between group members. Increasing the amount of socialisation between people can help to improve the quality of their lives. People with learning disabilities often suffer from poor physical co-ordination and all too often from visual impairment too. It is very important then, to reach out to these people and encourage them to interact with others. Anything which reduces a person's sense of isolation is beneficial. Music sessions are an excellent way of doing this.

6.2 Learning

A music session presents a great opportunity for learning. It is an ideal environment for introducing ideas because the group members are generally relaxed, happy and in a responsive mood. Reducing fears and anxieties, learning about the surrounding area and villages and speech improvement, are just some examples of the range of subjects which can be tackled.

Slides can be used during the sessions to great effect and present a new and different medium to the other more familiar visual media of television or films. Using slides, in conjunction with songs, helps people to understand the story told in the song. The slides also help to create special atmospheres linked to the words and/or meaning of the songs. An approach which creates learning possibilities is to build up sets of slides to work with. I took my own photographs and produced sets that included pictures of local villages and the landscape, pictures of mountains and the sea in Scotland, interiors of the little cottages making up a folk museum, and zoo animals. To avoid repetition, different sets of slides can be shown from one week to the next. By going over each slide slowly, for example the zoo animals, and naming the animal, some group members will learn the name of the animal and remember it the next time they are shown the same slide.

Slides can also serve to help reduce levels of fear and/or anxiety. For example, people who were afraid of dogs were encouraged to approach the screen and stroke the image of a dog. They subsequently appeared to be less anxious whenever they saw a real dog. Seeing pictures of the surrounding area and local landmarks helps clients to learn about them and to be able to identify villages etc.

Various theories have been put forward for teaching new songs but the following are straightforward guidelines, though some steps may be added, left out or rearranged to suit the particular requirements of a group.

1   Play the song several times, after an oral introduction if necessary.
2   Have the group hum the song or sing la, la, la.

3   Clap the rhythm before learning the words. If this goes well,
    move on to speaking the text rhythmically.
4   Sing the text.
5   Provide an accompaniment with percussion instruments if desired.

One musical aspect to introduce could be that of harmony. This was possible with one group consisting of two people, Maria and Julie. Both women were intelligent and Maria showed a definite aptitude for music. She had been taught the piano as a child and could read music. Often, when they sang together as a duo, harmonies would develop, usually at the end of a verse or phrase. Maria was usually responsible for creating the harmony but Julie managed to maintain the main tune while Maria sang the harmony.

The harmonies did not happen overnight. To begin with all three of us would sing together songs such as 'Now the day is over'. After we had sung a few verses or, more often, repeated the same verse a few times, I would sing in harmony with Maria and Julie. At first they would revert to what I was singing, but with gentle persuasion I managed to get them to sing the 'normal' tune and not to take any notice of me. We would then listen to the end result, played back on the tape recorder. They seemed to like the sound produced by harmony and occasionally Maria would harmonise on her own, the tape recorder playing the melody, to pleasing effect.

Encouraging people to learn new facts by using slides, introducing new songs and dances, and presenting plays all helps to increase interest in their environment and improve their learning skills. The results of an 18-week study supported this (see summary in Appendix A).

6.3 Concentration

Slides can also help in improving powers of concentration. Exercises can be devised in conjunction with slides for the purpose of identifying and spotting specified objects. Practice resulted in noticeable improvements. For example a set of slides showing a seagull flying in the sky or walking on the sand was used with the aim of playing 'spot the seagull'. In another example I arranged a set of slides which showed my Border collie dog, Sweep, rounding up a friend's flock of sheep. The pictures were taken without a telephoto lens, which resulted in Sweep appearing as a rather small figure in many of the pictures. However, he was visible and stood out from the sheep by virtue of his dark coat. Allowing each image to appear on the screen for a minute or two, I encouraged different people from the group to come forward to the screen and to try to point out where Sweep was on the picture. Those who appeared not to have a clue as to where he was had their hand moved gently to the correct position. They were then cheered and clapped, as much as those who had found Sweep on their own. The exercise seemed to be enjoyed by everyone.

6.4 Recognition

Developing abilities to recognise animals, objects or other people really depends on developing learning skills and powers of concentration at the same time. Repeated use of the same sets of slides will help individuals to learn to recognise and learn the names of animals etc. Slides of fellow group members and staff can be projected to improve the ability to recognise different people.

6.5 Co-ordination

Instruments such as the xylophone are good for improving co-ordination. By playing a xylophone someone can be encouraged not only to play a particular tune but also to do so to match a specified beat.

Speeding up or slowing down the beat requires greater concentration to keep the rhythm of the tune; this in turn demands greater control over the hands and arms so that the beater strikes the xylophone keys at the correct intervals in order not to break the rhythm.

If holding a xylophone beater is difficult or if hand-held instruments cannot be used, a rhythm can be created with hand bells or bells tied to the wrists or ankles. The rhythm itself is not so important here as the ability to maintain it and to change it when required to do so. It will be necessary to experiment with different instruments to find the best one for each person depending on their level of co-ordination.

6.6 Creativity

The music session may be the only outlet for group members to demonstrate their talents and creative skills and the leader should provide the utmost support and encouragement to any ideas participants may have. Creative skills often come to the fore during music sessions when people start singing or dancing spontaneously, of their own initiative, without prompting or initial encouragement from the group leader. Other skills include harmonising with the singing of other group members, and spontaneous comments made while acting in plays. It is important to show appreciation for any such efforts as this helps to build up confidence and expand the creative skills of those displaying them.

6.7 Communication

Communication between group members tends to increase just by virtue of being in a group playing musical instruments and singing together. Some people who are reluctant to talk, due to shyness or laziness, tend to avoid the use of speech if signs and nods or shakes of the head will suffice. However, people with Down's Syndrome sometimes find talking the least easy channel of communication compared to mime, sign, facial and body language. This is because their aural processing and expressive language develops more slowly than their visual processing and receptive language. People who can be encouraged to sing often progress to talking. It must be borne in mind that whether or not people talk depends very much on their immediate environment i.e. where they are and who they are with. In addition, when people with learning disabilities are slow to answer in conversation, other people often talk for them. Communication can also vary depending on how comfortable clients feel at the time.

It is important for the leader to know the usual level of communication displayed by clients in their day-to-day environment. Only co-workers who have daily contact with them will have that information which can sometimes be quite revealing. In one instance this was brought home quite forcefully to me, as illustrated in the following account. I had been asked by the resident consultant physician to pay particular attention to one member of the group and to try hard to develop his speech as he very rarely talked and when he did, it was in a barely audible whisper. I persevered for many weeks and eventually Neil uttered a few words. I was overjoyed and related this back to the co-workers who saw him on a daily basis. They were quite unimpressed telling me 'Neil talks all the time when he's with us on the unit!' Not only did he talk a lot, but he also had a fairly deep loud voice, particularly unexpected considering his small stature and his reluctance to speak in unfamiliar surroundings.

Chapter 7
DEVELOPMENT OF FULL POTENTIAL

7.1 Reading

The capability and speed with which new songs, tunes and words can be learned may vary enormously. However, many adults with   learning disabilities are able to read, having been taught at school, and this is a great advantage when learning new songs. The leader can print out song words and choruses in block capitals, photocopy them and hand them out. Great pleasure is derived from having one of these sheets and those who have a safe place to keep them can be given their own to keep. No-one ever forgot to bring their sheet with them to a session!

Another advantage is that many of the people concerned generally have little opportunity and/or motivation to read from one week to the next. However they tend to make every effort to concentrate hard and read the words on the sheet as they are so keen to learn the words to the songs.

It is worth noting that members who can read may come from groups exhibiting challenging behaviour and, equally, groups who do not. Generally, they will tend to be quick to learn, both in terms of music and dance. The incentive to practise reading helps to improve the ability to concentrate as well as the ability to learn.

As well as conventional music reading, alternative systems of music notation have been invented which may make it possible for some people with   learning disabilities to follow written music. Some of these schemes are based upon numbers one to eight to represent notes, others are based on letters. It is also relatively easy to devise colour codes to suit individual groups or individual participants.

7.2 Dance

While reading is sometimes an existing skill for some participants, dancing (apart from disco-dancing) usually is not. Dancing is easier to approach when the group is small in number. It is possible for one person to teach a group of 12, but it will take longer than if some help is available from a co-worker(s). It is best to concentrate on very simple dances, at least to begin with, while making allowances for the varying degrees of physical disability which may exist within the group. However, here again the mistake of assuming dance is out of the question for certain people because they do not look able to cope with it, has to be avoided. Michael, whose poor co-ordination made walking extremely difficult, and whose speech was incoherent and virtually non-existent, managed to perform two steps of the Breton dance described below. He needed very little encouragement and the minimum of guidance; he merely watched the leader's feet, then copied the movements. His movements were slow and jerky but the steps were perfect. The satisfaction he derived from being able to perform the dance was apparent as he clapped his hands and laughed.

A leader who initially does not know any dances can make some up. Very simple steps will do, but the dance must have sufficient structure to it to give the participants a sense of satisfaction when they manage to get it right. Everyone needs the sense of achievement which comes from striving to do something and finally succeeding. Experience has shown that involving people who often exhibit challenging or anti-social behaviour in dance can, in some cases, help them to socialise more easily with people in general, as well as with fellow group members.

I began with a Breton dance which I had learned while living in Germany. It comprises a very few simple steps, but is unusual in that it is performed in a sideways manner, rather than in a circle or facing your partner in any other fashion. As there were three of us in one instance I stood in the middle to guide them through the steps. *fig.7.1*

Starting with both feet together, the right foot steps about two feet to the right and the left foot then moves up to join it. This is now repeated. Again starting with both feet together, the left foot steps about two feet to the left and the right foot joins it, ending up with both feet together again. In effect, it is a case of taking two steps to the right and one step back to the left, which allows gradual but steady movement towards the right. This comprises the whole dance and can be repeated endlessly until the participants have had enough, are worn out or both! It is essentially a 'Long Dance' which should speed up with the music, ending with the dancers moving fairly quickly round a large hall, holding hands with a person on either side of them (except for the first and last person) and weaving in and out to avoid obstacles. The music should be in triple time.

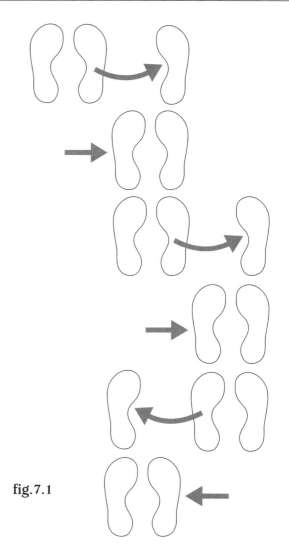

fig.7.1

Dances can also be made up based on existing known ones, or alternatively directly invented on the spur of the moment and tried out to see how well they work. One such made-up dance goes as follows.

Everyone joins hands to form a circle and dances clockwise for eight beats (simply counting up to eight), then they reverse direction and dance anti-clockwise, again for eight beats. The dancers then raise their right hand in the air, joining them together in the middle to form a 'star' and everyone dances eight beats clockwise. The direction is then reversed, everyone joining left hands in the middle again to form a 'star', and dances eight beats anti-clockwise. If the group consists of an even number of people, they can then form themselves into couples and, joining both hands with their partner, swing round for a count of eight beats, repeating this in the reverse direction. The dance is then ready to begin again. Any music which fits with the dance is appropriate, in this case music based on eight beats.

The main concern is to choose dances with the ability of the group members in mind. Rather than going into detail and outlining many different dances in this book, it would be better for the reader to get hold of a book about dances for further ideas.

As well as furthering socialisation, dance improves the ability of the participants to learn. It also gives everyone some exercise which, for those who receive little or no physiotherapy, can be invaluable. Progress will often be slow when teaching new dances, but patience will be well rewarded and the results are always worthwhile.

Chapter 8
THE VALUE OF THE TAPE-RECORDER

A small, compact, battery-operated tape-recorder, one that is easily moveable and which can be placed on the floor or on a table in the middle of the group is invaluable for recording the sessions. It is important for it to be inconspicuous though so as not to put off or intimidate performers.

The tape-recorder can also be used for sound-recognition games. It is suggested that sound fragments are not too long and it is best to begin with everyday sounds gradually building up to less familiar ones. There can be no definitive recommendation as to what to record but here are some ideas to get started:

doorbell
keys
cutlery
door slam
dog barking
cat mewing
telephone
vacuum cleaner
running water

Less common sounds:

unfamiliar animals
musical instruments
songs
car ignition
aeroplane
church bell
bicycle bell

There are a number of reasons for recording people singing and talking. It is surprising to discover that virtually no-one in most groups has ever heard the sound of their own voice, either singing or speaking, recorded before. The majority gain much pleasure from the experience and will request again and again to hear themselves singing.

Recording complete sessions by leaving the recorder running the whole time gives a good idea of how the session has gone generally. However, it also has the disadvantage of large wasted sections while dropped instruments are picked up from the floor, while performers take up their places to sing and so on.

Often I selected parts of the session to record, sometimes playing a song back immediately after it had been sung, and at other times playing back parts of the tape during a mid-session break, or at the end when we were putting the instruments away. It was not uncommon for someone to burst into spontaneous song, even when someone else was already singing at the time. This mostly happened with Brenda, a blind woman, who loved music and effortlessly memorised songs and tunes she had heard only once or twice before. Without any warning she would suddenly start singing a song or tune and I always did my best to record her whenever possible.

Hearing themselves on tape, apart from giving pleasure also helps with confidence in the ability to sing and helps provide greater motivation when it comes to their next attempt.

Again, results cannot be expected overnight. Reference to Appendix A (page 00) will illustrate how progress can be made one week, only to have apparently vanished the next, all too often a question of 'two steps forward, one step back'. However, with perseverance as the key, it is terribly important for the leader not to become down-hearted and believe efforts have been wasted; no effort can ever be wasted when dealing with people with   learning disabilities; in the long run they always benefit from music sessions, the contact with the leader alone providing a worthwhile experience.

The tape recorder can also be used to play pieces of music during a session, allowing the leader the freedom to move round the group and encourage participants to play their particular instruments. Pre-recorded pieces of music set to different rhythms can serve to illustrate rhythm changes and help group members follow these changes with percussion instruments.

A valuable session can be achieved using the tape recorder alone without the leader needing to play a single note! This is of particular benefit to non-musicians.

It is also useful to compare tape recordings of earlier sessions with more recent ones in order to assess the progress made by individual members and by the group as a whole. This enables the leader to make decisions about future sessions and to plan the direction these might take.

As mentioned in Chapter 3, recordings made during sessions can be used by co-workers to help generate or maintain an interest in the music, to provide a calming or stimulating effect on certain individuals and to enable songs and/or dances to be practised on an everyday basis.

Apart from the weekly anticipation of the forthcoming music session, having a long-term project to plan and prepare for can provide additional excitement in the lives of clients. Such projects can take the form of a musical play which can be developed with particular participants in mind. Appropriate cues can be provided by the leader when narrating the story surrounding the play. This serves as a way of prompting the 'actors' to 'do their bit' while lending continuity to the story.

Concerts may also be presented at regular intervals with the participants having several weeks to prepare their individual performances. Having a set date to aim for and making posters to advertise the event can generate much enthusiasm and excitement. Recruiting a reasonably-sized audience, and finding an area other than the usual one used for music sessions to hold the concert, will do much to enhance the feelings of satisfaction and achievement experienced by the participants.

MUSICAL PLAY

The method of presentation of the play is self-explanatory. Each person plays a part individually and/or within a group and all act on cues given by the group leader who narrates the spoken parts.

LONDON, LONG AGO

Spoken It was London in 1666 and the fire of London had just started to burn. Ellie happened to be walking through the streets when she saw flames coming from windows and roof tops and she started to sing.

['London's Burning']

Spoken Then a second person, Donald, also saw the flames of the fire of London and he sang too, to warn the people so that they could escape to safety.

[Donald comes on and joins in singing with Ellie]

Spoken Then another person, Cathie, came by and she too joined in with the singing.

[Cathie comes on and joins in singing 'London's Burning']

Spoken Then they went on their way leaving the fire behind them, back to their homes where they could be safe.

As they walked through the streets they passed Harold. He was standing on a street corner with a cap at his feet hoping people would drop money in so he could buy something to eat, maybe some roast chestnuts, on his way home. Ellie dropped some money in his hat as she went past, then Harold started to sing.

['Hallelujah']

Spoken Then Harold too, went on his way, taking his cap and money with him.

In the nearby market, two people were selling fish. They were Marjorie and Sydney, and as they stood by their market stalls they sang the familiar song.

['In Dublin's Fair City']

Spoken A lot was happening in the streets that day, Gerald, the world-famous clog dancer, happened to be in town, and did a wonderful dance display for passers by.

[Gerald dances to **'Boys of Malin'**

'High Road to Linton'. *Tunes played on the fiddle]*

Spoken   There were several taverns in London in those days and indeed there still are in the present day. A lovely version of 'Amazing Grace' could be heard drifting out of a pub doorway, sung by Jill.

*[Jill sings Verse **'Amazing Grace'**]*

Spoken   Then Jill went on to sing another song, **'John Brown's Body'**, everyone else in the tavern joining in after the 1st verse.

[Everyone joins in after 1st verse]

Spoken   Vinnie happened to be sitting near by in the tavern, and after Jill had finished singing he started to sing **'She'll be Coming Round the Mountain'**.

[Sings one verse]

Spoken   Then everyone else in the tavern joined in and of course the tavern 'sing song' would not have been complete without Sydney singing **'Lambeth Walk'**.

[Sydney sings Lambeth Walk]

Spoken   Finally, just before the tavern closed for the night, Adrian started to sing '**You are my Sunshine'**.

[sings one verse then everyone joins in]

Spoken   As people drifted out into the night leaving the warmth of the tavern behind them, they could hear a group of carol singers from across the street. It was Marjorie, Michael, Adrian and Jean singing 'Away in a Manger'.

['Away in a Manger'].

Spoken   Eventually the carol singers went home to their beds and the streets were deserted. Above in the sky, the stars twinkled brightly and very softly on the wind could be heard the voices of children going late to their beds and singing as they went the lovely song 'Now the Day is over

['Now the Day is Over'].

[Altogether 1st Verse, then Sydney's verse, then altogether 1st verse again]

Spoken   And then the singing gradually died away, and the town fell asleep.

THE END

Appendix A

SUMMARY OF THE WEEKLY REPORTS PREPARED BY THE AUTHOR CONCERNING MUSIC SESSIONS ON CHERRY WARD

The format over the 18 weeks that observations were made has included performing songs, both familiar and unfamiliar, playing tunes from many countries on the dulcimer, hurdy gurdy, fiddle and guitar, encouraging participation by way of dancing, singing, joining in with percussion instruments etc., and projecting coloured slides onto a screen, these including pictures from various parts of the British Isles, zoo animals, members of the group themselves, local villages, etc.

The aim of the sessions was to promote a feeling of well-being amongst group members, to stimulate the more subdued people and calm down the more excitable ones, to encourage participation and promote harmony in the group as a whole and, finally, to provide an environment for 1 hour a week in which they could enjoy themselves through music. This aim was achieved to quite a considerable extent. Over the weeks the more unruly members were seen to participate to a greater extent, tending to sit more within the group, wander about far less, and generally behave in a much calmer manner. The more subdued appeared to be very much stimulated by the music, in particular by the livelier tunes and the songs with a good rhythm. The degree of participation displayed by these members was seen to increase with the number of sessions they attended. The effects of the music continued after the session had ended, on some occasions with certain people singing songs that they had heard during the session. An increase in harmony generally between the different members of the group was also seen, and a degree of cohesion was apparent which was not present when the sessions began.

SUMMARY OF THE WEEKLY REPORTS PREPARED BY THE AUTHOR CONCERNING MUSIC SESSIONS ON NEWHOUSE WARD

The format over this 18-week period included performing songs, playing tunes on the dulcimer, hurdy gurdy and fiddle, showing coloured slides on a screen (including pictures of the group members) but, in particular, encouraging individuals to sing songs on their own and/or recite poetry, to learn new songs and, lastly, to learn steps to a Breton dance.

The aim of these sessions was to improve the self-image of the participants, in addition to increasing their confidence in their ability to do things. Also, it was hoped that this newly acquired confidence might be transferred to everyday activities outside the session, leading to a greater display of initiative. Another aim of the sessions was to promote a greater degree of harmony amongst group members, particularly when considering that a certain amount of anti-social behaviour was displayed by them generally on a day-to-day basis. Finally, the sessions were aimed at providing everyone with an hour's enjoyment that they could look forward to every week.

A surprisingly high degree of success was obtained with this group that would not have seemed possible at the beginning. Three people in particular, Julie, Maria and Patricia benefited greatly from the sessions and displayed a remarkable change in behaviour during them. This was particularly evident with Maria, who regularly attacked other group members during the earlier sessions, but later developed into a friendly, enthusiastic person. She readily learned new songs and perfected the steps to a Breton dance, as well as showing a much higher degree of tolerance towards the other group members. Julie also changed for the better, tending to sing at a normal volume, rather than reciting poems very loudly at inopportune moments. Both Julie and Maria began to sing together readily, in addition to performing the Breton dance, which required them being in close proximity, something which would not have been possible to attempt when the sessions began. Patricia also became much calmer and participated, using instruments, actually becoming an integral part of the group, whereas earlier on she was very much an outsider.

Appendix B

MUSIC

The type of music used in sessions is open to the discretion of the leader. The author chose examples of tunes from the Celtic tradition, which can be readily found in Celtic music books.

Some lent themselves well for dancing while others were excellent as the central melody for percussion accompaniment. (The 'Dance of the Bear' is ideal for the Breton dance and can be found in Chapter 7.)

The author also made use of her own compositions during music sessions and a selection of these songs has been included in the centre pull-out section.

References

Whinnom, Alex, *Let's Make Music*, Manchester: Printforce, 1989.

Wood Miriam, *Music for Living [enriching the lives of profoundly handicapped people].*
Kidderminster: British Institute of Mental Handicap, 1982.

Bibliography

Hooper, J., 'Music hath charms....', *Nursing Times*, Vol. **87**, No. 37, September 1991.

Oldfield, Amelia and Feuerhahn, Carol, 'Using Music in Mental Handicap: 3 – Helping young children with handicaps and providing support for their parents', *Mental Handicap*, Vol. **14**, March 1986.

Oldfield, Amelia and Parry, Carol, 'Using Music in Mental Handicap: 1 – Overcoming communication difficulties', *Mental Handicap*, Vol.**13**, September 1985.

Oldfield Amelia and Peirson Janet, 'Using Music in Mental Handicap:
2 - Facilitating movement', Mental Handicap, Vol. 13, December 1985.

Whinnom, Alex, *Let's Make Music*, Manchester: Printforce, 1989.

Wood, Miriam, *Music for Living [enriching the lives of profoundly handicapped people].*
Kidderminster: British Institute of Mental Handicap, 1982.

Index